# The Cutting Room Floor

# The Cutting Room Floor

by Sherrie Ball

**Rebirth Ink**
**Milwaukee, Wisconsin**

Copyright © 2013 by Sherrie Ball

All rights reserved. This book or any portion thereof may not be reproduced or used in any manner whatsoever without the express written permission of the publisher except for the use of brief quotations in a book review.

Printed in the United States of America

First Printing, 2013

ISBN-13: 978-0615843674
ISBN-10: 0615843670


Rebirth Ink
Milwaukee, WI 53225

rebirthink@gmail.com

# Table of Contents

## Preface

## Section One
| | |
|---|---|
| The Fabric | 3 |
| Melancholy | 4 |
| Trapped | 5 |
| Gossamer Lie | 6 |
| Mundane | 7 |
| Fallen | 9 |
| Before the Cimmerian Night | 10 |
| Legitimacy | 11 |
| The Passing | 12 |

## Section Two
| | |
|---|---|
| Anybody Home? | 13 |
| The Plea | 14 |
| The Unsaid | 15 |
| The Gamble | 16 |
| Flat Line | 17 |
| Reliance | 18 |
| The Sum | 19 |

## Section Three
| | |
|---|---|
| Silk Purse | 20 |
| Coveted Word | 21 |
| Knowledge | 22 |
| Soldiers' Lament | 23 |
| Hear Me | 24 |
| Honor | 25 |
| I Do Not Know Your Name | 26 |
| The Value of Love | 27 |
| Acceptance | 28 |
| The Dove | 29 |

| | |
|---|---|
| The Cutting Room Floor | 30 |

## Section Four
| | |
|---|---|
| Sorrow | 31 |
| Rat of Despair | 32 |
| He Patiently Waits | 33 |
| Letting Go | 34 |
| One Day | 35 |
| The Inheritance | 36 |
| The Photograph | 37 |
| Falling Star | 39 |
| Penalty of Love | 40 |
| Faith | 41 |
| Undying Love | 42 |
| The Door | 44 |
| What's Left | 45 |
| Angels | 47 |
| Live Your Life | 48 |
| Amy | 49 |
| Loves' Breath | 51 |

## Section Five
| | |
|---|---|
| I Think | 52 |

# Preface

I consider myself to be an emotional writer. As
such, I often scribble on scratch paper
trying to understand me and the world in which I
am included.
I have found that in divulging those sentiments with
others there is a commonality that
links many of us as humans. When I think I must be
the only one, I find myself one of a multitude of
people who feel as I do. I have realized that readers
can connect to my words, as language spoken in
their hearts, that they cannot themselves express on
paper.

This book of poetry surrounds the revealing of the
past seven years of frustration, guilt, discovery,
loss, and faith. These years of my middle age when
I have become more aware of; what I have and have
not accomplished, what I have gained and lost, what
I have discovered and have yet to learn. It is the
same journey we all must face between
birth and death.

The eldest of eight children; I have been writing
since I was a small child growing up in the rural
community of Strawberry Point, Iowa. I now reside
in Prairie du Chien, Wisconsin, a single mother who
has raised three grown children, and has a child
with special challenges still at home. Other poets
would consider my style of writing as New
Formalism. I regard it as old school. Principally, I
compose metered poetry that rhymes.
Quite simply, that is how the expressions come to
me.

## Acknowledgment

This book is dedicated to the angel that whispers in
my ear from Heaven, my niece,
Andrea Bockenstedt (1993-2007) and the angels
God gave my care to, my loving
parents, Robert and Diane Keppler.

"I once thought the compass of the world set its'
sight by me. Now I realize the direction
that life takes you does not set itself by you alone.
Instead, also by the course of those
who surround you and sometimes, by the universe
itself." - Sherrie Ball

## The Fabric

I think the world is a loom,
my brain the weft,
words the warp
that create the fabric
I cloak myself.

## Melancholy

There is nothing
as deceiving as
hope;
nor as truthful as
despair.

## Trapped

Confined
with all I have enclosed.
Cornered
by hounds in my brain.
Restrained
dreams that will not become.
Caged
by fear, my private pain.
Caught
in pressure of my design.
Ensnared
by that I do not require.
Suffocated
the sorrow that I drown.
Entombed
the coffin of my desire.
Trapped
reality of my barrier.
Lured
by promise on gilded hook.
Restricted
the diversity to control change.
Imprisoned
by excuse from which I took.

## Gossamer Lie

Oh how wicked the beauty of a spiders lair-
captivating the dew caught upon her snare.
The moth that is wrapped now flutters in fright
sought in the dark now searches for light.

Entranced are we gossamer truth and lies
as she suckles the blood who hears the moth cry?
The splendor is wicked upon the net we weave
cobwebs in our head stay— no reprieve.

Wind rushes upon the frailty, yet the knot holds fast
the mesh we create to future, from past.
The Labyrinth remains our hearts' still wrapped
as the moth that is glued to the spider clings
trapped.

We grapple each thought till' it creates a net of our lives
each strand leaving wonder, distance between sighs.
Like a leaf that is captured as it danced in the breeze
threads becomes tangled to become
the web that we weave.

## Mundane

I wonder when the precise moment was
when the abnormal became ordinary
the unexpected, routine.

When mine became the house
with the window that everyone else peers into
and sees people walking on ceilings,
talking to walls.

I wonder where that time went
when I worried about small things
like burnt cake,
the price of gas,
paying the bills.

The concerns of a "normal" person,
with "normal" lives,
in "normal" homes,
with "normal" children.

That don't require
steady doses of intrusion to:
measure,
dose,
break,
mend,
scan,
record,
probe,
analyze,
and draw the blood of,
and extract something of,
the regular.

At least I can remember
the commonplace,
the run of the mill,
my son never will.

## Fallen

There is a place that holds like humid air.
Time that has no end. A position that does not care.
A dwelling never finished. Panes forever closed.
If I exist within, my neighbors will never know.
A future needs design. A past, replaced
if I could free myself from this space.
I have choices to choose, decisions to decide,
laughter to smile, tears to be cried.
The place waits in caution for the green light to glow,
as the traffic is jammed with no place to flow.
A place with no heaven. A place with no hell.
Into the hollow of limbo—

I fell,
I fell,
I fell.

## Before the Cimmerian Night

In the dawn he arises to ask,
"who is this man reflected in glass?"
Within the jungles shadow steps his lonely soul
as he searches the sun through his sepulchral hole.

Friend to few, enemy to some
he mistrusts love— devotes to no one.
Concealing from all especially, from he
sometimes he stares as if to see-

where he was—who he is
does it matter what this day gives?
Like shrapnel scars dull pain drives
he covers his existence between truth and lies.

Daring the executer he lives on edge
his voids departure or let him live.
In the dusk he passes the mirror
his image reversed he does not peer.

He subsides beyond the glass—
undefined between present and past.
To an unknown force fatigue draws sleep
outstretched in supplication he reaches for release,
yet he awakens to the morning light
hoping peace may find him—
before the Cimmerian night.

## Legitimacy

When does being considerate of others' cross the
line to become a lie?
When the person you are born to be begins to
slowly die?

When you are afraid of being silenced so you don't
speak at all?
When you are fearful to take a step because you
don't want to fall?

When you are so terrified of losing that you won't
put up a fight?
When you're scared of being called wrong
so you don't stick up for what's right?

When you're anxious someone won't like you
    if they find out who you really are?
When you're worried to go the distance because
that may be too far?

When you cry yourself to sleep because of
confusion you can't evade?
When you find yourself apologizing sooner than
fault was made?

You can never be truly loved if no one knows the
actual you.
If they can't accept that person does it matter at all
if they do?

You only perjure yourself if consideration you use
to justify.
The legitimacy to ensue your truth— then becomes
your lie.

## The Passing

Perhaps life is simply
a transitory place
between the birth of your soul
the death we must face
between what we discover
or experience of mind
between what we must lose
for what we will find
between famine and riches
war and release
greed and hunger
generosity and peace
between tears and laughter
hurt and wellbeing
from walking with blinders
then actually seeing
between evil and honest.
between what is said and done
beyond our ego
to share what is won
between what waits
or what we have given
between just existing
to truly living
between the cherubs of heaven
beyond hounds of hell
are the choices we make
for where we must dwell
perhaps life is simply
a transitory place
between the birth of your soul
with the death we must face.

## Anybody Home?

We all open
the door of our heart
to a different sound.
For some a soft bell.
Others, a repetitive chime.
For many—
it may take
some real hard
knocks.

## The Plea

Everyone's soul seeks completion.
It does not search for perfection—

Instead, the kindling that nurtures a pier
That will endure the flame of time.
It longs for that single individual
That will preserve friendship,
Balance lassitude,

Believe—
Without constraint,
That they are the only person
That is meant to be with them
For eternity.

The true match will withstand trial.
Advance past obstacle.
Answer beyond death, the plea
Of one heart to another
Return its' rhythm
To the place it longs.

# The Unsaid

You seemed so far away
yesterday.
Though, you sat right there
in your chair
two feet
between you and I
was no where.
You would stare at the
television.
I would speak words
Unheard.
Only to my brain,
where I am fluent
in all matters unsaid.
Dead
you and I.
Envy, for those
who reach one another
through miles,
over years,
beyond death.
Never crying the chasm
of the television and
no where.

## The Gamble

We played a game you and I
I was sure I could win
The cards were dealt
The bets were made
The contest would begin.
We laid our cards one by one
Then we placed our bet
I gambled on love
Thinking that I
Would be the one to collect.
But your poker face was better than mine
I couldn't read you at all
It wasn't long
Before every one of
My chips began to fall.
Eventually, you called me out
The truth was finally told
Love doesn't win
Collect your wager
I fold.

## Flat Line

When love finds you,
your pulse quickens.
When love stays with you,
it finds a steady beat.
When love leaves you,
it must stop.
If only—
a brief moment,
to reset its' measure
once again.

## Reliance

I am so exhausted of pursuing someone
who has no desire to be caught.
A name who would rather hound
phantoms of his past than to exist
in the present with me.
A person who is so desolate he desires
drugs, alcohol or death rather than
receive affection he feels unworthy of.
I must understand that he refuses
outcome and will live in his sorrow
till' the earth swallows him in anguish.
I must realize that I cannot amend his
perception of life— only for the value of love.
It may be adequate that love is not enough.
"Being" is simply what it is for that moment
nothing to be completed. For I can decide
no ones direction, then put aside my own.

## The Sum

What price is it I must pay
The cost of trust—
the sum of pride
loss of respect I feel inside
The value of myself
I offer away
the penalty of love
to have you stay?
I am covered at night
Beneath the blanket of despair
extending a nightmare
that departs to nowhere.
What worth does it hold
the significance of words
when the call that disputes
the only echo that is heard?
What is the sum of a soul
when the substance is stolen?
How much must I give
by the end of the day—
for the penalty of love
what price must I pay?

## Silk Purse

I am no silk purse.
I am not dainty, or fancy.
I do not carry
Only the space
Wanted for vanity.
I am a burlap bag.
I am strong and durable.
I can hold the burden
Of heavy loads,
For the necessity of many.

## Coveted Word

The blood of those who
fought for independence
in the Revolutionary War,
still pulses within
the soil of America.

The tears of the bereaved
continue to sustain
the parched spirits of
every war beyond that
our time has begotten.

Pay tribute to all those
who have suffered the cause,
to justify the most coveted
of all words—
Freedom.

## Knowledge

I was roused like the bud
of the foundling tree in spring
A fresh life full of promise
in my awakening.
Years fled, winds changed
As I reached toward the sky
though, I had not the wisdom
as the aged, Old Oak nearby.
I was happy to have shed
the seed that opened from earth.
I put beyond me, the past
from which came my birth.
Till' the copious shade of days
began descending to the ground
left me barren in recognition
the knowledge, Old Oak had found.
Now I can welcome the changes
in the seasons of my time,
to appreciate the seasons
from the juncture that is mine.

## Soldiers' Lament

Once, I wore a scarlet tunic
With shoes in leather gleam
I strode with every belief
For my obliged British regime
As the days turned to months
The months to years, beyond
My tunic now ruddy brown
To wind and weather respond
My boots carry break and blister
Hunger is all that fills
Disease of mind and body
Impartial— to its' kill
Yet I find another battle
I move toward cannon fire
Again, I find my tempo
The composition— artillery choir
When this contest finds its' winner
No man will have prevailed
For all that conflict gives upon
Only heartaches are unveiled
For my longings are as every soldier
To each warrior call the same
With no distinction, color of garment
Our cries echo a similar name
Carry me home and give me peace
Anon, the waking of the dawn
I ask no more— obtain no offer
The combats before us and gone
We soldiers will ever' pursue
This day and forever beyond
As our command must find us
We continue to march along
Carry on.
Carry on.

## Hear Me

When I bid you, listen to me
but you start granting advice.
you have not done as I've requested.

When I ask you to listen to me
then you begin to advise me why
I shouldn't feel that way,
you are treading on my feelings.

When I require you to listen to me
instead, you believe you must
resolve my problem, you have
neglected me.

So please listen and attend me.
Then, accordingly, at your
request I will
listen.

## Honor

Freedom is more than an anthem
You cannot simply, sing its' praise.
We shouldn't measure our liberation
Released—
By those who have paid.

# I Do Not Know Your Name

I do not know your name—
Nor for which battle you died.
I do not know your home,
Nor the tears that were cried.

I do not know where you rest—
Nor the promises broken.
I do not know your uniform
And your fears lay unspoken.

But, I know your spirit exists—
That your courage is admired,
And your sacrifice is honored
By each soul that's inspired.

And I offer you from my heart
Thank you, to guardians unknown
For offering yourselves for us all
That we may keep freedom...
Our home.

Bless you

## The Value of Love

I have never mourned the loss
of a treasure chest buried deep,
nor do I remember the face of money
when I'm haunted in my sleep.
My family never sat at a counting table
when we blessed our meal each day.
I don't recall asking Dollar Bill
to come outside and play.
When comfort was my neediness
a buck never wrapped me in embrace.
My most important memories
didn't happen at Prosperity Place.
The gift I hope to offer my children
in material gain cannot be found.
Our wealth is inside our family circle
not within cash, possession, nor ground.
To me there are no riches greater
than the strength my family offers.
If given the choice of love or coin
I would sooner be buried a pauper.

## Acceptance

If I had to choose
between being loved or accepted,
I would choose to be accepted.
Although, love shows affection,
devotion & desire;
acceptance shows approval,
tolerance & belief.
I know many who say they love
that do not accept.
Love can constrain.
Sometimes, by its' very nature
it can hold conditions.
Acceptance always allows freedom.
Freedom to forgive & be forgiven;
tolerate and be tolerated,
give and receive,
allow and be allowed,
for simply,
being
exactly who you are.

## The Dove

I could hear the dove calling
soft coos beckoned me
from the pink, blossomed branches
of the laden apple tree.
I didn't want to hear him.
I covered my head,
concealed in the shadows
neath' the pillow on my bed.
I tried to keep the dove silent
with his offering of peace.
I wanted to ignore
any promise of release.
In the comfort of the nest
I had once felt at ease.
But, I fell to the ground
with the promise of a breeze.
Yet, he sings ever softly
never quitting this chant—
Get up. Soar with me.
for though, you abandon yourself
God can't.

## The Cutting Room Floor

As I scatter the remnants of young age to the film
of my middle aged floor, I have uncovered within those
cylinders of time the unraveled spools of filament
before, and throughout, my existence.

As I crawl among the film scavenging the images
that compose the character I am at this moment I seek
in desperation for the exact method to advance my prospect
featuring in celebrated roles.

I seek those clips for which I was beautiful,
generous, and
gorged with hope. I sever those cuts in which I was repulsive,
gluttonous, and filled with hate. Then, I arrange carefully the
performance that I intend to expose into view the
balance of my life.

## Sorrow

A person feels loss not
in one dominant moment.
Instead, in countless
inferior moments that
are indifferent
to any etiquette
of grief.

## Rat of Despair

Grief
Is the chameleon
Of emotions
It disguises itself as
Jealousy— love
Anger— hatred
It changes people into
Someone they were not
Someone they don't recognize
A person they were not meant to be.

Grief
Can make you forget everyone
In its' consumption
It is the snake that unhinges
The jaw and swallows
Happiness
Faith
Hope.

Grief
Is the rat of despair
The scurry in the dark halls
Of the mind
It scavenges upon
The very last crumb
Of your heart
To leave in its' gluttony
Nothing—
But the place you used to be
And the person
You will never be again.

## He Patiently Waits

I avoided the spectacle, not desiring to face the assailant.
His stench drifted through the corridor.
I detected him approaching in the echoes of the hall.
I suffered his scuttle across my skin—
leaving paths of crawling flesh. I witnessed him when I opened the door. I understood that he felt solace,
tranquil in this transitory place. He examined our facade—
drawing the oxygen away, seeking to strangle her breath.
She realized he was present, a smile on her desiccate lips,
trepidation in her gaze. He plucked away her attractive curls.
Withered her hide to expose bone. Left her pierced with his barbs.
Offered hostile tumors to nurture inside her.
He mutilated her with venomous toxin. Assigned her to implore—
liberation from her torment. Her outer shell, frail, and ancient.
The significance of time in her visage.
She pleaded to live, implored to die; interrogated the Messenger, why?
I couldn't wait to flee the place, though I suffered remorse,
she consented and whispered, goodbye.
I knew she imprisoned her tears. Upon my leave I glanced in observance,
She held a Pepsi in her left hand—
Death, embraced her right.

## Letting Go

Yours was the hand that held mine
to keep me safe and to reassure.

Yours was the hand that held mine.
to offer me comfort when I was unsure.

Yours was the hand that held mine.
when I was sick or when I was in pain.

Yours was the hand that held mine.
the hand of reason when I needed refrain.

Yours was the hand that held mine
the strength when I didn't feel strong.

Yours was the hand that held mine
the support when the world felt wrong.

Mine is the hand that holds yours
desperate that you should know
that your hand in mine is precious—
I don't want to have to let go.

## One Day

Someday—
she thinks the shroud will lift
and she'll awaken to the warmth of the sun.
Someday—
she thinks I'll walk out of the darkness
this morning is just not the one.
Someday—
she thinks my spirit won't be heavy
and my steps will, once more, be carefree.
Someday—
she thinks I might know who I'm looking at
when I stare at that person who was me.
Someday—
she won't breathe with the ache in her chest
and her heart won't constrict with pain.
Someday—
she will move beyond that one day
that has made everyday since, the same.
Someday—
she thinks she'll move past the grief
and enjoy the life around her.
Someday—
she thinks she'll exist in the present
instead of remembering where they once were.
Someday—
she thinks I won't be depressed
and my eyes will ignite with a smile.
Someday,—
she thinks I'll be normal again,
but, that someday
just may be awhile.

## The Inheritance

Whoever said, "It is better to have loved and lost
than to never have loved at all."
has never endured the death of a child
suffering the betrayal of God's merciless call
has not been thrown aside by a nation
a defiled symbol of a finished war
left to solicit life on the streets
to survive as freedoms' whore
never clutched the decay of abuse
nor carried the doubt of self worth
been born to want love from a parent
having only felt despised since birth
has never survived in wretched poverty
ingested by the bile of despair
disregarded by a civilized world
that is too self enlightened to care
never devoted themselves to a man
to find they married violence and shame
given only the offer of fear in return
for the privilege of submissions name
it may be better to never feel loves burden
it is an emotion that deceives
sometimes, a wound that never heals
will be the only inheritance in its leave.

# The Photograph

The picture
confines her smile.
Silence.
I reach to touch.
Remote, remorseless.
My fingers caress
the frame.
Pain traces me.
Her joy beckons.
I try to answer.
Inwardly,
I die.
I beg the Lord
to offer her back,
allow her to appear
from the photograph.
Stillness,
my reply.
No warmth do I feel.
My arms empty,
reaching for contact
never to be mine again.
Emptiness swallowed me.
Choking on my heart.
Devouring happiness.
Conquering the person
I once was.
Leaving me to a life
of coping.
But, I will smile for you
simply,
as the image
looks at me.
Nothing existent

except, a glimpse
of who I used to be.

## Falling Star

I saw you in the sky last night
that flaming star surpassing night.
I could reach my hand to feel
the love that gives your spirit light.
The universe must always expand,
yet the world diminishes its extent.
It keeps you near, yet far away
that unbound place, where you went.

You were here to ignite our existence,
to crash our lives with boom and basin.
Now you travel to infinite places
leaving only a trail of illumination.

You awed us all with your presence.
Your force still gives display.
For you were born a falling star,
to show us splendor, then soar away.

## Penalty of Love

Grief
follows the trail of lost tomorrows
it inhales the breath of escaping sigh.

Grief
pursues the trail of masquerade
it is the thief that steals your alibi.

Grief
feels the trembling you hold within
it savors the salt of the un-cried tear.

Grief
lingers past the time of endurance
and knows the falsehood of your veneer.

Grief
is the thief that steals your choice
it is the sleep that cannot be sedated.

Grief
claims the loss of every sorrow
because we love— the sum is equated.

**Faith**

I have faith
that each departed spirit
I have loved will
attend me while
I remain on earth,
then stand before God
beside me, as a witness
when the day comes
that I am judged.

## Undying Love

Sometimes— it is not the right time
Sometimes— there is more to be done
Sometimes— there are words to be said
Sometimes— I had to be the one.

Yesterday — I was not prepared to leave
Yesterday— I had hugs to give
Yesterday— I had a future to plan
Yesterday— I had to live.

Once in a while— you can stretch a season
Once in a while— you can hold a smile
Once in a while— you can battle and win
If once in a while— is only, "once in a while."

Today— the respite felt right
Today— the earth seems to know
Today— I am going to make peace
Today— I am preparing to go.

Tomorrow— will behold another day
Tomorrow— you will need to be strong
Tomorrow— will spill tears for us
But tomorrow— your life will go on.

I wish— I could have remained longer
I wish— I could comfort your fears
I wish— it were my decision to make
I wish— we could have counted more years.

To— those I adored, you gave my life purpose
To— my family you carry my heart
To— my love a part of my soul lives within you
To all— carry my memory and we'll never part.

One day — I will embrace you again
One day— I promise we will be together
One day— you will feel me at your side
One day— you will know my love did last
—Forever.

## The Door

Do not consider
The door as closed
For when I left my body
My spirit arose.

My soul survives
It breathes beyond time
Past earthly moments,
Out of my bodies confine.

Still, I understand you.
I soothe your tears.
I realize your pain.
I quiet your fears.

I listen silently
While you speak to me.
I cradle you in my arms
As sadness flees.

I hear your laughter,
Encourage your dreams,
Motivate your triumphs,
Inspire your esteem.

We stay separated,
But a little while,
Till' then provide me
The joy of your smile.

I am within your heart
Just unlock the door
It will remain open
For you evermore.

# What's Left

I ran through purple clover,
Sending butterflies to the sky.
I have held a newborn kitten
With silken fur and sleepy eyes.

I have galloped in the wind
On a horse that was in flight.
I have curled into a sleeping bag
Beneath the stars at night.

I have savored in the feel of mud
As it squished between my toes,
And watched with awe the firefly
As in the night it glows.

I have laughed so hard my tummy
Would protest in its pain.
I have shared so much joy
That I know some will remain.

I have been loved so deeply
That it reaches through to me.
I was content with my home
So my heart was always free.

I lived life for each moment
Not measured by a clock.
I never gave a worry on,
When death would come to knock.

My life was always bursting,
So when I left it was fulfilled.
I never lost the dreams
That age will sometimes kill.

You can experience a lifetime
In only thirteen years,
Or die after a long life
Never reaching past your fears.

You leave fragments of yourself behind
From the moment of your birth.
So what will remain of you I ask,
When you leave this earth?

The life you entrust is not determined
By merely its stretch alone
But how you were aware of each day here
And the happiness you've known.

*Written on behalf of my beautiful niece, Andrea.*

## Angels

Angels are—
The whispers you hear
When not a word is spoken.

Angels are—
The hope that you keep
Though your heart is broken.

Angels are—
The hand on your shoulder
If shadow's cross your way.

Angels are—
The light you will find
Even on the darkest of days.

Angels are—
Those souls who speak
Beyond, a life past.

Angels are—
Existent through time
Because, love never breathes its' last.

## Live Your Life

I am beside you in every moment
I exist wherever you go.
I am the candle burning within
I am your hearts, gentle glow.
Your sorrow caresses me,
As icy fingers in frozen snow.
I can meet you in happiness
It is a place I love to go.
I can hear you speak to me
It flows as whispers toward night.
I can feel your anguish
As I am hugging you tight.
Life is a gift ever fleeing
A second cannot be replaced.

Live Your Life

With that, I am embraced.

# Amy

Amy was just a little girl
When the nightmare awakened her.
Her mother came into her room—
Said, morning will welcome you soon
Then tucked her back into bed.

She whispered, "close your eyes Amy
God will chase the nightmare away."
Then, the child danced with angels
A butterfly, in God's Ballet.

Amy was just a little girl
When her head began to ache,
Her father held her in his arms—
Tried to soothe away her harms
As he stroked her unruly, red curls.

He said, "relax your eyes child
God will dry the tears away."
Then Amy began to calm
As her father began to pray.

Amy was just a little girl
When she lost all her wild curls,
Struggling, was all that she knew
But her faith and trust grew
As Amy's parents held her close.

Her parents promised, "sleep now Amy
God will meet you in the sun
He will take away your anguish
Before this day is done."

Amy was just a little girl

When her body grew too tired,
She searched for the light.
Her body gave up its fight—
An angel carried her away.

The angel spoke, "awaken now Amy,
As your spirit passes the gate—
To enter upon God's Kingdom
Where His loving arms await."
A new angel was born.

## Loves' Breath

I believe love
Does not leave us
When we part from this earth
It offers to embrace us
Before the moment of our birth.

I believe love
Lives beyond departure
To awaken hearts that would sleep
Beyond the glass of memories
To give shatter, despairs keep.

I believe love
Comforts us during nightmares
In remembrance, holds our hand
Binding the strength— a single fasten
To carry the weight of a strand.

I believe love
Matures past all ages
During time yet to befall
Peering through, to view an epoch
That has yet to build its wall.

I believe love
Does not sink entombed
You do not bury it with your death
It is that one thing that forever endures
Love, survives by its' own breath.

## I Think

I think some things need to change so we appreciate what is constant.

I believe some of the best illusionists are not as famous as Criss Angel, but are instead, simple people who show the world a brilliant smile when inside themselves they cry and no one ever recognizes their deception.

I think you can starve your soul dwelling upon all that has gone wrong in your life. But, you can feed your soul reflecting upon all that is good.

I believe that Humanity is the child of Empathy. If you never have, or lose, the ability to understand another person's pain, Humanity will die and Empathy's sister, Selfishness becomes fertile and bears the child, Inhumane.

I think everyone knows people who are surrounded by others and live their lives in nearly total isolation.

I think people tend to believe that being happy shouldn't take any effort and can become extremely discouraged when they are not. I believe that being happy requires work and ambition. It is despair that is effortless and ready.

I think relationships are like cooking, in that you can't master its art without failing a few recipes.

I think it is hard not to wonder how much fate a person inherits and how much is created, because in that answer you will know how much you can change and how much is beyond your will.

Time and Love...I think nothing can be both as forgiving and unforgiving as these.

I think misery must finally collapse a person's view to one thing, to find pleasure in their life again.

I think some people are so self-absorbed they become like a sponge that's over saturated and can't soak up a single tear for anyone else.

I think the best thing about unconditional love is that no matter what, you love. I think the worst thing about unconditional love is that no matter what, you love.

I think I went to bed last night with the day half finished and awakened this morning to find the day half gone.

Speaking for myself, self-pity and depression are NOT the same. The waters of depression are murky and hold terrible creatures. In that case if you care about someone enough all you can do is jump in and try to hold their heads above that bog, until the monster lets go of their ankle.

I think people need faith as much as love. Faith in a higher power, other people, the future, yourself. I can't think of anything more despairing or lonely then having faith in nothing and no one.

I think it may be okay to believe "the grass is greener on the other side" if it serves as motivation on breaking barriers, and not an excuse for getting your head caught in barbed wire.

I think the truths we are concealing the most from ourselves are often considered the most visible to everyone else that knows us.

I think it a shame that we must spend such a great portion of our lives maintaining what we already have, that we make such little time to construct something new.

I think everyone is born to teach humanity something whether that life is lived 10 minutes or 110 years; It may be love, patience, forbearance, forgiving, empathy, fear, appreciation, wariness, friendship, knowledge or a million other things. Every life has an affect on someone's life in some way, so each life must leave an effect in its absence.

I think that generally speaking I am pretty good at reading people. That said, some people are like books filled with interesting dialogue and others are blank between the front & back cover.

I think that more than anything I despise lying; to me it's cowardly. The only satisfaction I get out of a liar is watching that thread of deception they thought to use as an escape; tangle round. Too late, they always find out the truth they sought to betray is the binding force that chokes them.

I think when you have traveled the same road with the same person for awhile and your partner abandons the vehicle any of these can happen; you can pull up at an intersection not knowing which direction to take; you can pick up hitch hikers and keep circling the same rutted road around and around; you can stall your engine and never move forward; you can push the gas and run over anyone in your path, or you can junk what carried the two of you altogether, salvage yourself and walk with steadiness, wherever the road ahead leads.

A good sign a relationship is finished is when you begin to put "room" in front of "mate" in your mind.

# Rebirth Ink
## Milwaukee, Wisconsin

Rebirth Ink is a Milwaukee based, small press publisher whose current portfolio and forthcoming publications are not defined by any particular genre but rather by the distinction and quality of the writing. We are looking for new or previously published authors, poets and playwrights whose writing is substantial and displays a firm grasp of their chosen craft.

Rebirth Ink offers critique and editing services to assist authors from conception to manuscript. The words are there, inside you. Let us help you find them.

**For details,
forward questions or query letters to**

Rebirth Ink, Milwaukee, Wisconsin at rebirthink@gmail.com

Printed in Dunstable, United Kingdom